SALVATION IN CHRIST
The Total Package

Bisi Peter

SALVATION IN CHRIST
The Total Package

Bisi Peter

Copyright © September, 2020

CONTENTS

INTRODUCTION

Christianity is a call to responsibility. What you do would determine what result you get, which invariably determines your salvation. As the foundation is very vital for any building that must stand, so is your Christian growth and maturity. The depth of your Christian foundation would determine how long and strong you can stand in the faith.

How you start your journey in God is very important. Just imagine your father is the president of a university and because of that you choose not to complete a high school and sit for the entrance examination into the university which is the basic criteria for securing admission into a higher institution. However, because your father is the university president doesn't guarantee admission into the university. You cannot secure the admission except your father doesn't want to be a good role model.

Jesus Christ, our perfect role model didn't just start his ministry and start healing the sick and doing all the great work we read about in the Bible. He built up from a foundation. He started from the ground up to becoming so powerful. He started by always going to the mountain to pray. He fasted for forty days and forty nights. All these were the building process for a solid foundation, which help Him fulfilled destiny.

When a Christian has a good and solid foundation in Christ, exploit becomes very easy. A wise man once said *your root determines your fruit.* If you observe, any time there's a serious storm, you will see some trees on the ground and when you take a closer look at the ones that fell and the ones still standing you will discover that the difference is in their depths. The ones still standing are always deeply rooted than the ones on the ground. If you don't want to be on the ground when the storm of life comes, you must be deeply rooted. Storms are the best test of depth.

Chapter 1

EMPOWER FOR DOMINION AND POWER

What is the value of Christianity if you are not dominating? Before God created man he had already activated dominion for him. *"And God said, Let us make man in our image, after our likeness: and let them have dominion over the fish of the sea, and over the fowl of the air, and over the cattle, and over all the earth, and over every creeping thing that creepeth upon the earth"* — Gen 1:26.

Life without dominion is frustration. Life without dominion is shame. The devil doesn't have a problem with you because you gave your life to Christ. Rather, the devil begins to get frustrated when you exercise power and dominion. By default you are supposed to have dominion and power.

Now here is what the bible says about power: *"Behold, I give unto you power to tread on serpents and scorpions, and over all the power of the enemy: and nothing shall by any means hurt you."* —Luke10:19.

Power and dominion are for spirit not flesh. Immediately you surrender your life to Christ, you begin to operate in power and dominion. However, operating with power and dominion starts with identifying who you are. The question now is, Who are you? What is man?

Man is a spirit that has a soul and lives in a body. I often ask this question every time, have you seen God before? You are thinking right? Don't worry, the answer is simple: *"God is a Spirit: and they that worship him must worship him in spirit and in truth."* —John 4:24.

Immediately you surrender your life to Christ, you cease to be human being (flesh) you become a spirit being living in a physical tent and directed by the Holy Ghost whom you have surrendered your spirit. Man's spirit is a free agent and can yield to any spirit. Yielding your spirit to the spirit of God makes you one with the Holy Spirit.

A man of God once gave a testimony of his dominion and power over witches and wizards. After preaching one day, he made an altar call for witches and wizards and they stood up.

He asked one of them, what do you do?

The witch replied, "We suck blood."

Where? The man of God asked.

"On the highway sir." The witch answered.

The man of God continued: "What would you do if peradventure you are on the highway sucking blood and somebody like me approaches?" The witch replied, "We leave the high way."

Now, that's power and dominion been exercised. You don't suck power and dominion except the witch wants to dry up. They can suck the blood in the flesh but certainly not the spirit blood, because spirits don't have blood.

You must understand that blood differs. The difference start with the question of who are you. You must understand that ye are gods (Psalm 82:6).

Identifying your personality is vital if you must dominate and exercise power. You must identify who you are and stay true to your identity. You don't say who you are and try to hide that fact when circumstances arise. Jesus speaking to the Jews about who he was said, "I and my Father are one". And because he identified himself they wanted stoning him. Then he asked them, "What exactly are you stoning me for?" They replied, "For good work we stone you not, but for blasphemy you made yourself equal to God." Jesus answered them saying, "Is it not written in your law, I said, Ye are gods?" —John 10:30:34 (paraphrased)

You must understand that you are a god and gods only dominate and exercise power. We all know that the Most High God cannot give birth to the most low rat. We are not redeemed to be a failure and every child of God is a seed of Abraham and generational symbol of greatness. A child of a Lion is another Lion even though some say he is a cub, but he will grow up to become a Lion.

Let this understanding stick in you: power and dominion doesn't come by talking nor by wishing. If wishes were horses, beggars would ride. Power and dominion comes by working. Jesus Christ before he started dominating and exercising power fasted for forty days and forty nights. Remember, He was always going to the mountain to pray and also doing several other spiritual exercises. All these are examples of work. Little wonder he was dominating evil spirit and casting them up and down. Even His garment was healing the sick, etc.

Take a closer look at any powerful personality in Christ frustrating the devil and his cohort. It's usually on the basis of work, exercised in faith—not bread and butter Christian. Work of faith gives rise to dominion and power, while wish equal to faithlessness.

A good example of work is recorded in Mark 4:37-41 saying: *37 And there arose a great storm of wind, and the waves beat into the ship, so that it was now full. 38 And he was in the hinder part of the ship, asleep on a pillow: and they awake him, and say unto him, Master, carest thou not that we perish? 39 And he arose, and rebuked the wind, and said unto the sea,*

Peace, be still. And the wind ceased, and there was a great calm. 40 *And he said unto them, why are ye so fearful? How is it that ye have no faith?* 41 *And they feared exceedingly, and said one to another, what manner of man is this, that even the wind and the sea obey him?*

The above scripture exemplifies power and dominion at work. A short prayer that was backup with work gave an instant answer 'peace be still.'

In the same vein in the book of Acts 19:6-8, we see how Paul turned around situation by works. The scripture says: 6 *And when Paul had laid his hands upon them, the Holy Ghost came on them; and they spake with tongues, and prophesied.* 7 *And all the men were about twelve.* 8 *And he went into the synagogue, and spake boldly for the space of three months, disputing and persuading the things concerning the kingdom of God.* This is a direct result of work.

However, people of wish do things differently: 13 *Then certain of the vagabond Jews, exorcists, took upon them to call over them which had evil spirits the name of the Lord Jesus, saying, We adjure you by Jesus whom Paul preacheth.* 14 *And there were seven sons of one Sceva, a Jew, and chief of the priests, which did so.* 15 *And the evil spirit answered and said, Jesus I know, and Paul I know; but who are ye?* 16 *And the man in whom the evil spirit was leaped on them, and overcame them, and prevailed against them, so that they fled out of that house naked and wounded." —Acts 19:13-16*

Before God created man, he already gave him dominion and power but man lost this dominion and power to sin.

The only thing that can take away power and dominion is sin. But what exactly is sin? Sin is Satan in nature or Satan identification number. All unrighteousness is sin: and there is a sin not unto death (1 John 5:17).

Consequences of Sin

(1.)   Death.
The end plan of the devil for any child of God is death.

> *23 For the wages of sin is death, but the gift of God is eternal life in Christ Jesus our Lord.*
> —Romans 6:23.

(2.)   You are separated from God.

> *1 Surely the arm of the LORD is not too short to save, nor his ear too dull to hear. 2 But your iniquities have separated you from your God; your sins have hidden his face from you, so that he will not hear.*
> —Isaiah 59:1-2.

(3.)   Poverty, your heavens is closed.

9 "You expected much, but see, it turned out to be little. What you brought home, I blew away. Why?" declares the Lord Almighty. "Because of my house, which remains a ruin, while each of you is busy with his own house.
10 Therefore, because of you the heavens have withheld their dew and the earth its crops.
—Haggai 1:9-10.

(4.)   Sickness.

58If thou wilt not observe to do all the words of this law that are written in this book, that thou mayest fear this glorious and fearful name, THE LORD THY GOD;

59Then the LORD will make thy plagues wonderful, and the plagues of thy seed, even great plagues, and of long continuance, and sore sicknesses, and of long continuance.
—Deuteronomy 28:58-59.

Man was designed for eternity, but sin happened and man died.

19 In the sweat of thy face shalt thou eat bread, till thou return unto the ground; for out of it wast thou taken: for dust thou art, and unto dust shalt thou return.
—Genesis 3:19.

But thank God for Jesus that came to correct the first mistake Adam and Eve made. Jesus came for the remission of sin. The Bible says that *...He was wounded for our transgressions, he was bruised for our iniquities: the chastisement of our peace was upon him; and with his stripes we are healed.* —Isaiah 53:5

What does it means to be born again? It is being reborn in the spirit. The scripture is clear on this: *5 Jesus answered, Verily, verily, I say unto thee, Except a man be born of water and of the Spirit, he cannot enter into the kingdom of God. 6 That which is born of the flesh is flesh; and that which is born of the Spirit is spirit.* —John 3:5-6.

Privileged Benefits of Being in Christ

(1.)   Liberty: You are free from sin.

1 Stand fast therefore in the liberty wherewith Christ hath made us free, and be not entangled again with the yoke of bondage
—Galatians. 5:1

(2.)   No condemnation:

1 There is therefore now no condemnation to them which are in Christ Jesus, who walk not after the flesh, but after the Spirit.
—Romans. 8:1

(3.)   Empowered by God for dominion and authority:

19 Behold, I give unto you power to tread on serpents and scorpions, and over all the power of the enemy: and nothing shall by any means hurt you.
—Luke 10:19

(4.)   Right of Son-ship:

12 But as many as received him, to them gave he power to become the sons of God, even to them that believe on his name.
—John 1:12.

(5.)   Ye are god:

6 I have said, Ye are gods; and all of you are children of the most high.
—Psalm 82:6

In Christianity, repentance is not an option. It is a must for any Christian that must dominate and reign in power, that was why Peter advised them to repent: *37 Now when they heard this, they were pricked in their heart, and said unto Peter and to the rest of the apostles, Men and brethren, what shall we do? 38 Then Peter said unto them, Repent, and be baptized every one of you in the name of Jesus Christ for the remission of sins,*

and ye shall receive the gift of the Holy Ghost —
Acts 2:37-38.

Repentance is a must for any foundation that will stand. The keyword is repent and the first step to going about that is to say this short prayer. You must mean everything you say:

Lord Jesus, I have come to you today, knowing that I am a sinner. I believed you died and rose on the third day in victory. I surrender my life to you. Be my lord and saviour. Take control of me. From this day forward I turn my back on sin and receive your grace to walk with you all the days of my life. Right now, I believe I am justified by your blood and I'm now a child of God.

Thank you Lord for saving my soul.

Amen.

Chapter 2

THE WORD OF GOD

Immediately you know who you are in Christ Jesus, then the next step is to begin to speak like gods. Everything created was by the word of God. The word of God is the foundation for everything, the word of God is God himself. The scripture says: *In the beginning was the Word, and the Word was with God, and the Word was God —John 1:1.*

Heaven and Earth were not created by blocks or cement, but by the word. *And God said, Let there be light: and there was light* (Genesis 1:3). The word of God is the foundation for any Christian that will live a triumphant life. Every building that will last requires a solid foundation, so is every Christian that will mature and abide in the kingdom.

The bible is not an historical account of God's dealing with man, but it's God's make-up for man's victorious and fulfilled living.

Through faith we understand that the worlds were framed by the word of God, so that things which are seen were not made of things which do appear.
—Hebrews 11:3

Life is a journey, to get to your destination you need a map, and that map is the word of God. Here's an illustration: a man bought a gadget sealed in a carton. Immediately he got home, he opened the gadget and started trying to operate it instead of learning how to operate it from the manual that came with the gadget. Most people go in this direction. But look carefully, you will find an instruction called a manual containing guidelines on how to operate the gadget. A wise man once said what the fool does in the end, the wise person does in the beginning. In journeying through life, the manual is the word of God.

The word of God is your life manual on how to operate in this world. It contains your purpose on earth and why God created you. Birds don't struggle to fly; fishes don't struggle to swim. You ought not to struggle to live a triumphant life. Any time you are struggling, it means you are walking against God's purpose for your life.

What is the word of God?

The scripture says, *"In the beginning was the word, and the Word was with God, and the Word was God"* —John 1:1. The word of God is God himself. There is no difference between me and my word. The word of God of is a manual. It is a standard operating procedure for all

Christian. Again, *16 All scripture is given by inspiration of God, and is profitable for doctrine, for reproof, for correction, for instruction in righteousness: 17 That the man of God may be perfect, thoroughly furnished unto all good works* (2 Timothy 3:16-17).

The word of God is in two dimensions: logo and rhema. Understanding these concepts is very important when it comes to the word of God. Logo is the written will of God to his children, which is contained in the Bible. The Bible is a package God delivered to man in a written form. It can also be called the letter (2 Corinthians 3:6). Rhema on the other hand is the spoken and the quicken word of God. It is the spirit and life behind the word. It can also be called revelation.

Why You Need to Study the Bible

1. It produces faith.

    17 So then faith cometh by hearing, and hearing by the word of God.
    —Romans 10:17

2. It reveals Jesus Christ.

    18 Search the scriptures; for in them ye think ye have eternal life: and they are they which testify of me.
    —John 5:39

3. It make wise unto salvation.

15 And that from a child thou hast known the holy scriptures, which are able to make thee wise unto salvation through faith which is in Christ Jesus.
—2 Timothy 3:15

4. It profits.

15 Meditate upon these things; give thyself wholly to them; that thy profiting may appear to all.
—1 Timothy 4:15

5. It brings perfection.

17 That the man of God may be perfect, thoroughly furnished unto all good works.
—2 Timothy 3:17

How to Study the Word of God for Your Profiting

When it comes to studying the word of God for your profiting, the perfect example is Mr. Goat. If you take a closer look at a goat when his eating, the Goat start by chewing the cud then swallow the cud. After a while, most especially when the Goat is relaxing, he vomits the cud back (regurgitate) and then re-chew it. From my observation, I believed the process that the Goat re-chews the cud is the most important. I also believe that the cud the Goat vomit and re-chew is the one that profit the Goat's body. This is how the word of God walks. It isn't about just reading the word but going over it (re-chewing) again and again and making it a part of you.

Now here are the under-listed ways of studying the word of God.

Reading: When you read the word of God the best place it can be is your head.

16 Seek ye out of the book of the Lord, and read: no one of these shall fail, none shall want her mate: for my mouth it hath commanded, and his spirit it hath gathered them.
—Isaiah 34:16

13 Till I come, give attendance to reading, to exhortation, to doctrine.
—1 Timothy 4:13

Hearing: When you continue hearing the word of God, it will stay in your mind.

17 So then faith cometh by hearing, and hearing by the word of God.
—Romans 10:17

Studying: When you start studying the word of God, it moves from your head to your heart.

15 Study to show thyself approved unto God, a workman that needeth not to be ashamed, rightly dividing the word of truth.
—2 Timothy 2:15

Meditating: Mediation entails pondering when you meditate on the word of God it move from your head to your heart and you get revelation and that is when the profiting comes.

8 This book of the law shall not depart out of thy mouth; but thou shalt meditate therein day and night, that thou mayest observe to do according to all that is written therein: for then thou shalt make thy way prosperous, and then thou shalt have good success.
—Joshua 1:8

15 Meditate upon these things; give thyself wholly to them; that thy profiting may appear to all.
—1 Timothy 4:15

Frequent usage:

14 But strong meat belongeth to them that are of full age, even those who by reason of use have their senses exercised to discern both good and evil.
—Hebrews 5:14

Sharing the words:

17 Iron sharpeneth iron; so a man sharpeneth the countenance of his friend.
—Proverb 27:17

24 There is that scattereth, and yet increaseth; and there is that withholdeth more than is meet, but it tendeth to poverty.
—Proverb. 11:24

Things to Avoid so You Can Profit from the Word

Slothfulness: If you are slothful, you miss your slot.

9 How long wilt thou sleep, O sluggard? When wilt thou arise out of thy sleep? 10 Yet a little sleep, a little slumber, a little folding of the hands to sleep:

11 So shall thy poverty come as one that travelleth, and thy want as an armed man.
—Proverb 6:9-11

Sin:

1 Behold, the LORD'S hand is not shortened, that it cannot save; neither his ear heavy, that it cannot hear: 2 But your iniquities have separated between you and your God, and your sins have

hid his face from you, that he will not hear.
—Isaiah 59:1-2

Distraction:

Distraction are side attraction seeking attention, if you want to profit from the word avoid distraction when studying the word of God. Put away all forms of distractions and respect the King of Kings.

25Therefore I say unto you, Take no thought for your life, what ye shall eat, or what ye shall drink; nor yet for your body, what ye shall put on. Is not the life more than meat, and the body than raiment?

26 Behold the fowls of the air: for they sow not, neither do they reap, nor gather into barns; yet your heavenly Father feedeth them. Are ye not much better than they?

27 Which of you by taking thought can add one cubit unto his stature?

28 And why take ye thought for raiment? Consider the lilies of the field, how they grow; they toil not, neither do they spin:

29 And yet I say unto you, That even Solomon in all his glory was not arrayed like one of these.

30 Wherefore, if God so clothe the grass of the field, which to day is, and to morrow is cast into the oven, shall he not much more clothe you, O ye of little faith?

31 Therefore take no thought, saying, What shall we eat? or, What shall we drink? or, Wherewithal shall we be clothed?

32 (For after all these things do the Gentiles seek:) for your heavenly Father knoweth that ye have need of all these things.

33 But seek ye first the kingdom of God, and his righteousness; and all these things shall be added unto you.

34 Take therefore no thought for the morrow: for the morrow shall take thought for the things of itself. Sufficient unto the dayisthe evil thereof.

—Mathew 6:25-34

Materials needed for Effective Study of the Word of God

- Complete bible.
- Different bible versions.
- Bible dictionary.
- Table and chair.
- Pen.
- Note book.

Things wouldn't just work because of the personality involve, but it will walk because of the principles apply.

24And when he was entered into a ship, his disciples followed him. And, behold, there arose a great tempest in the sea, insomuch that the ship was covered with the waves: but he was asleep.

25 And his disciples came to him, and awoke him, saying, Lord, save us: we perish.

26 And he saith unto them, Why are ye fearful, O ye of little faith? Then he arose, and rebuked the winds and the sea; and there was a great calm.
—Matthew 8:23-26

Chapter 3

FAITH THAT WORKS

The Bible defines faith as the substance of things hoped for, the evidence of things not seen (Hebrew 11:1). Faith can also be defined as a living force drawn from a living word which produces living proof(By bishop David oyedepo). It is also a spiritual force that connects the mortal man with the immortal God. Lastly, faith is a display of confidence in God and his word until a desired result is obtained. The word says in Hebrews.10:35-36, *"Cast not away therefore your confidence, which hath great recompense of reward. For ye have need of patience, that, after ye have done the will of God, ye might receive the promise."*

When fear knocks at the door, faith opens and sees no one there. Faith is like electricity you can't see it but you can see the light. In the school of faith, your sight is irrelevant. You don't need to see anything. All you need to do is to believe. When you begin to see everything with your sight, you begin to lose your insight.

Putting confidence in a man is like chewing with a sore tooth or trying to run with a broken foot according to John Mason.

*⁵ Thus saith the LORD; Cursed be the man that
trusteth in man, and maketh flesh his arm, and
whose heart departeth from the LORD.
⁶ For he shall be like the heath in the desert, and
shall not see when good cometh; but shall inhabit
the parched places in the wilderness, in a salt
land and not inhabited.*
—Jeremiah 17:5-6

It is not because things are difficult that we do not dare, it's because we do not dare that things are difficult.Tell me who is your best friends and I will tell you who you are. If you run with wolves you will learn how to howl, but if you associate yourself with eagles you will learn how to soar.

*¹⁷ Even so faith, if it hath not works, is dead,
being alone.
¹⁸ Yea, a man may say, Thou hast faith, and I
have works: shew me thy faith without thy
works, and I will shew thee my faith by my
works.*
—James. 2:17-18

Faith that is mixed with works is faith that works. You cannot just be chatting faith without backing it up with work. When a good capacity of work is mixed with faith the result is inevitable.

There is this testimony of a woman that listen to her pastor preaching about faith the pastor said if you have faith like a mustard seed you can say to this mountain be thy remove and be move to yonder and will not doubt in your mind it will be done. And the woman believes and there is this mountain behind the woman's window stopping her ventilation and immediately, she got home that day, she said to the mountain, O ye mountain my pastor said if I have faith as mustard seed I can say to this mountain be thou remove and move to yonder. Therefore, O ye mountain be thou remove in the name of Jesus and after a while the woman was wondering why the mountain is still there.

She was so angry, that she went back to the pastor, and said why did you lie to me? I spoke to the mountain and the mountain is still standing there; why? And immediately, the pastor said the mountain is no more there, immediately you spoke to the mountain it moved but the problem is your eye, you have a sight problem called doubt.

The pastor continued: Faith believes. It is a substance of things hope for, the evidence of things not seen. The woman was confused the more. She went back and after some days some expatriate came to the woman and said Madam, please, there is something under this mountain we need to take off, but we are paying you for the inconvenience. The mountain was taken off and at the end of the day she was duly compensated

Immediately she spoke, the mountain left but her doubt was the problem.

13 If ye then, being evil, know how to give good gifts unto your children: how much more shall your heavenly Father give the Holy Spirit to them that ask him?
—Luke 11:13

The level of your faith determines the level of your work.

Levels of Faith

No faith or Zero faith: When you express so much fear about a situation, it means you lack faith in God. See illustration in the scripture below.

37And there arose a great storm of wind, and the waves beat into the ship, so that it was now full.
38 And he was in the hinder part of the ship, asleep on a pillow: and they awake him, and say unto him, Master, carest thou not that we perish?
39 And he arose, and rebuked the wind, and said unto the sea, Peace, be still. And the wind ceased, and there was a great calm.
*40 And he said unto them, **Why are ye so***

Little faith: Faith of this nature is expressed when you make a move of faith and suddenly you begin to develop doubt in your heart, which begin to drown your move of faith. See illustration in the scripture below.

Great faith: Great faith believes in the word of Jesus and acts accordingly with doubt in the heart. See an illustration of a great faith below.

them that followed, Verily I say unto you, I have not found so great faith, no, not in Israel.
—Matthew 8:8-10

25 Then came she and worshipped him, saying, Lord, help me.

26 But he answered and said, It is not meet to take the children's bread, and to cast it to dogs.

27 And she said, Truth, Lord: yet the dogs eat of the crumbs which fall from their masters' table.

28 Then Jesus answered and said unto her, O woman, great is thy faith: be it unto thee even as thou wilt. And her daughter was made whole from that very hour.
—Matthew 15:25-28

Nothing is more impactful like your example. Lastly faith is so important, that even God is not pleased if faith is not in place. His word is clear on this. It says, *"But without faith it is impossible to please him: for he that cometh to God must believe that he is, and that he is a rewarder of them that diligently seek him."* — Hebrews. 11:6

Faith without work is dead.

17 Even so faith, if it hath not works,is dead, being alone.

18 Yea, a man may say, Thou hast faith, and I have works: shew me thy faith without thy works, and I will shew thee my faith by my works.

19 Thou believest that there is one God; thou doest well: the devils also believe, and tremble.

20 But wilt thou know, O vain man, that faith without works is dead?

21 Was not Abraham our father justified by works, when he had offered Isaac his son upon the altar?

22 Seest thou how faith wrought with his works, and by works was faith made perfect?

23 And the scripture was fulfilled which saith, Abraham believed God, and it was imputed unto him for righteousness: and he was called the Friend of God.

24 Ye see then how that by works a man is justified, and not by faith only.

25 Likewise also was not Rahab the harlot justified by works, when she had received the messengers, and had sent them out another way?

26 For as the body without the spirit is dead, so faith without works is dead also.

—James. 2:17-26.

Chapter 4

THE PREVAILING PRAYER

If God is actually your father then calling home wouldn't be a problem because a soundless Christian is a sign less Christian. It takes sound to make a sign. The devil smiles when we make plans. He laughs when we get too busy, but he trembles when we pray. Don't worry about anything instead pray about everything. Time spent in communion with God is never lost. The highest purpose of prayer is not to change your circumstance but to change you.

Prayer may not change all things for you but will surely change you for all things. God is waiting to hear from you. Call him. He says, *"Call unto me, and I will answer thee, and shew thee great and mighty things, which thou knowest not."* —Jeremiah 33:3

What is the value of prayer if there is no answer? Life will not give to you what you deserve but what you demand on the prayer altar. A wise man once said, what you don't know ask, even if you know confirm whether what you know is correct.

¹And it came to pass, that, as he was praying in a

certain place, when he ceased, one of his disciples said unto him, Lord, teach us to pray, as John also taught his disciples.

2 And he said unto them, When ye pray, say, Our Father which art in heaven, Hallowed be thy name. Thy kingdom come. Thy will be done, as in heaven, so in earth.

3 Give us day by day our daily bread.

4 And forgive us our sins; for we also forgive every one that is indebted to us. And lead us not into temptation; but deliver us from evil.
Luke 11:1-4

What is Prayer?

Prayer is a call to God. His word says, *"Call unto me, and I will answer thee, and shew thee great and mighty things, which thou knowest not."* —Jeremiah 33:3. Also, in Matthew 7:7, it says, *"Ask, and it shall be given you; seek, and ye shall find; knock, and it shall be opened unto you."* Indeed, prayer is a call to God's throne room.

Prayer is two-way communication between God and man. It is talking to God and hearing from God. It is an act of asking and receiving from God.

Prayer is **ACTS.** The acronym stands for:
A - Adoration
C - Confession
T - Thanksgiving
S - Supplication

Prayer is asking God to intervene in a giving situation on the basis of His word. It is your confession at the point of confusion and your conclusion to that condition.

Prayer must be carried out without ceasing.

[17] Pray without ceasing —1 Thessalonica 5:17

Misconceptions about Prayer

Prayer is not just asking without hearing or receiving. There is a reason God gave you the mouth and added the ear. There's no communication if the other party is not responding.

It is not complaining and telling God about our problems. Instead of telling God about your problem do the opposite and tell your problem to be careful you have a mighty God. Remember: *"For after all these things do the Gentiles seek:) for your heavenly Father knoweth that ye have need of all these things."* –Matthew 6:32. We must be guided with the word of God.

It's not begging God to do things for us. God isn't mad at us. He's always ready to work with us and make us whole. He says, *"Come now, and let us reason together, saith the LORD: though your sins be as scarlet, they shall be as white as snow; though they be red like crimson, they shall be as wool."* —Isaiah 1:18.

Barriers to Effective Prayer

Sin and Disobedience: Sin is a sinker. It's either you deal with it or it deals with you, and if you are not careful, it will sink your destiny. See how sin affects God's children: *"Behold, the LORD'S hand is not shortened, that it cannot save; neither his ear heavy that it cannot hear. But your iniquities have separated between you and your God, and your sins have hid his face from you, that he will not hear."* —Isaiah 59:1-2. Even when you don't act it: *"If I regard iniquity in my heart, the Lord will not hear me."* —Psalm 66:18.

Praying amiss: Praying amiss is asking wrongly. Your intentions for asking from God must be good. It must be for a right cause. God's word is clear on this in James 4:3. It says, *"Ye ask, and receive not, because ye ask amiss, that ye may consume it upon your lusts."*

Pride:

12I fast twice in the week, I give tithes of all that I possess.

13 And the publican, standing afar off, would not lift up so much as his eyes unto heaven, but smote upon his breast, saying, God be merciful to me a sinner.

[14] I tell you, this man went down to his house justified rather than the other: for every one that exalteth himself shall be abased; and he that humbleth himself shall be exalted.
—Luke 18:12-14

Doubt and fear:

[6] But let him ask in faith, nothing wavering. For he that wavereth is like a wave of the sea driven with the wind and tossed.
[7] For let not that man think that he shall receive any thing of the Lord.
[8] A double minded man is unstable in all his ways.
—James 1:6-8

Bitterness/murmuring:

[10] Neither murmur ye, as some of them also murmured, and were destroyed of the destroyer.
—1 Corinthians 10:10

Lack of gratitude: An ungrateful heart of prayer never receives answers.

[41] Then they took away the stone from the place where the dead was laid. And Jesus lifted up his eyes, and said, Father, I thank thee that thou hast heard me.

⁴²And I knew that thou hearest me always: but because of the people which stand by I said it, that they may believe that thou hast sent me.
⁴³ And when he thus had spoken, he cried with a loud voice, Lazarus, come forth.
⁴⁴ And he that was dead came forth, bound hand and foot with grave clothes: and his face was bound about with a napkin. Jesus saith unto them, Loose him, and let him go.
—John. 11:41-44

Ingredients of Prayer

Be focused and specific:

¹¹ Give us this day our daily bread.
—Matthew 6:11

⁴⁷ And when he heard that it was Jesus of Nazareth, he began to cry out, and say, Jesus, thou Son of David, have mercy on me.
—Mark 10:47

Fasting: Fasting boost the believer's spiritual alertness and sensitivity to God. Fasting makes your prayers faster. When you fast you feed the spirit.

³ And Jehoshaphat feared, and set himself to seek the LORD, and proclaimed a fast throughout all Judah.

7 Art not thou our God, who didst drive out the inhabitants of this land before thy people Israel, and gavest it to the seed of Abraham thy friend for ever?
—2 Chronicles 20:3/7

16 Go, gather together all the Jews that are present in Shushan, and fast ye for me, and neither eat nor drink three days, night or day: I also and my maidens will fast likewise; and so will I go in unto the   king, which is not according to the   law: and if I perish, I perish.
—Esther 4:16

21 Howbeit this kind goeth not out but by prayer and fasting.
—Matthew 17:21

Locate the relevant word to the situation of need.

1 LORD, remember David, and all his afflictions:
—Psalm 132:1

Faith:

1 Now faith is the substance of things hoped for, the evidence of things not seen
—Hebrew 11:1

Pray in the spirit:

¹² For we wrestle not against flesh and blood, but against principalities, against powers, against the rulers of the darkness of this world, against spiritual wickedness in high places.
—Ephesians 6:12

How to Pray

(1.) Prayer must be directed to the Father in Jesus name:

⁹ After this manner therefore pray ye: Our Father which art in heaven, Hallowed be thy name.
-Matthew 6:9

¹⁰ That at the name of Jesus every knee should bow, of things in heaven, and things in earth, and things under the earth;
-Philippians 2:10

(2.) Confess your sins:

¹⁸ If I regard iniquity in my heart, the Lord will not hear me:
-Psalm 66:18

¹ Behold, the LORD'S hand is not shortened, that it cannot save; neither his ear heavy that it

cannot hear:
[2] But your iniquities have separated between you and your God, and your sins have hid his face from you, that he will not hear.
-Isaiah 59:1-2

(3) Hallow his name, praise him, worship him and thank him:

[1] Make a joyful noise unto the LORD, all ye lands.
[2] Serve the LORD with gladness: come before his presence with   singing.
[3] Know ye that the LORD he is God: it is he that hath made us, and not we ourselves; we are his people, and the sheep of his pasture.
[4] Enter into his gates with thanksgiving, and into his courts with praise: be thankful unto him, and bless his name.
-Psalm 100:1-4

[25] And at midnight Paul and Silas prayed, and sang praises unto God: and the prisoners heard them.
-Acts 16:25

(4) Be kingdom oriented in your prayer:

[33] But seek ye first the kingdom of God, and his righteousness; and all these things shall be added unto you.
-Matthew 6:33

(5)   Ask according to His will:

14 And this is the confidence that we have in him, that, if we ask any thing according to his will, he heareth us:
-1 John 5:14

(6)   Ask in faith. Having known what God says in His word.

27 And when Jesus departed thence, two blind men followed him, crying, and saying, Thou Son of David, have mercy on us.
28 And when he was come into the   house, the blind men came to him: and Jesus saith unto them, Believe ye that I am able to do this? They said unto him, Yea, Lord.
29 Then touched he their eyes, saying, According to your faith be it unto you.
30 And their eyes were opened; and Jesus straitly charged them, saying, See that no man know it.
-Matthew 9:27-30

You must understand that God answers prayer. Your responsibility is to pray. God says open your month wide and I will fill it.

10 I am the LORD thy God, which brought thee out of the land of Egypt: open thy mouth wide, and I will fill it.
-Psalm 81:10

[28] Say unto them, As truly as I live, saith the LORD, as ye have spoken in mine ears, so will I do to you:
-Numbers 14:28

Chapter 5

KINGDOM SERVICE

God first gave man what to do before he showed him what to eat. The garden you don't keep and dress is not permitted to offer food to you. When you stop making contribution to your world, you are no longer living but merely existing. Christianity is a call to service and inside your service is your glorification. The whole essence of the Christian walk is for the promotion of God's kingdom.

Kingdom service is using or putting your given talent, strength, resources, time, finances etc. to promote and expand God's kingdom on earth.

18 For through him we both have access by one Spirit unto the Father.
-Ephesians 2:18

18 Being then made free from sin, ye became the servants of righteousness.

19 I speak after the manner of men because of the infirmity of your flesh: for as ye have yielded your members servants to uncleanness and to iniquity unto iniquity; even so now yield your members servants to righteousness unto holiness.
-Romans 6:18-19

You cannot be working in Barclays Bank and be expecting payment from Bank of America. That is to say, you can only earn or eat from where you work.

Why must I serve God?

You must bear fruits as God expects:

¹ I am the true vine, and my Father is the husbandman.
² Every branch in me that beareth not fruit he taketh away: and every branch that beareth fruit, he purgeth it, that it may bring forth more fruit.
-John 15:1:2

It is a commandment:

⁴ I must work the works of him that sent me, while it is day: the night cometh, when no man can work.
-John 9:4

¹⁷ But Jesus answered them, My Father worketh hitherto, and I work.
-John 5:17

It is a privileged to contribute your quota

in the building process.

It is an expression of your love for him:

30 And thou shalt love the Lord thy God with all thy heart, and with all thy soul, and with all thy mind, and with all thy strength: this is the first commandment.
-Mark 12:30

3 And Solomon loved the LORD, walking in the statutes of David his father: only he sacrificed and burnt incense in high places.
-1 King 3:3

You cannot love without giving. If you claim you love God your love must answer the supreme test question.

Which are?
(i.)   The supreme test of discipline-ship.
(ii.)   The supreme test of conduct.
(iii.) The supreme test of service.

15 So when they had dined, Jesus saith to Simon Peter, Simon, son of Jonas, lovest thou me more than these? He saith unto him, Yea, Lord; thou knowest that I love thee. He saith unto him, Feed my lambs.
16 He saith to him again the second time, Simon, son of Jonas, lovest thou me? He saith unto him, Yea, Lord; thou knowest that I love thee. He saith

unto him, Feed my sheep.
17 He saith unto him the third time, Simon, son of Jonas, lovest thou me? Peter was grieved because he said unto him the third time, Lovest thou me? And he said unto him, Lord, thou knowest all things; thou knowest that I love thee. Jesus saith unto him, Feed my sheep.
-John 21:15-17

How to Serve God

(1.) Prayer of intercession (standing in the gap)

God's kingdom:

33 But seek ye first the kingdom of God, and his righteousness; and all these things shall be added unto you.
-Matthew 6:33

God's servant:

10 So Joshua did as Moses had said to him, and fought with Amalek: and Moses, Aaron, and Hur went up to the top of the hill.
11 And it came to pass, when Moses held up his hand, that Israel prevailed: and when he let down his hand, Amalek prevailed.

12 But Moses' hands were heavy; and they took a stone, and put it under him, and he sat thereon; and Aaron and Hur stayed up his hands, the one on the one side, and the other on the other side; and his hands were steady until the going down of the sun.
-Exodus 17:10-12

(2.)   For others:

10 And the LORD turned the captivity of Job, when he prayed for his friends: also the LORD gave Job twice as much as he had before.
-Job 42:10

a. Evangelism (Soul Wining)

30 The fruit of the righteous is a tree of life, and he that winneth soul is wise.
-Prov. 11:30

35 Say not ye, There are yet four months, and then cometh harvest? Behold, I say unto you, Lift up your eyes, and look on the fields; for they are white already to harvest.

36 And he that reapeth receiveth wages, and gathereth fruit unto life eternal: that both he that soweth and he that reapeth may rejoice together.
-John 4:35-36

(3)   Serve God With Your Means (Finance and Materials)

³⁸ Give, and it shall be given unto you; good measure, pressed down, and shaken together, and running over, shall men give into your bosom. For with the same measure that ye mete withal it shall be measured to you again.
-Luke 6:38

¹⁰ Bring ye all the tithes into the storehouse, that there may be meat in mine house, and prove me now herewith, saith the LORD of hosts, if I will not open you the windows of heaven, and pour you out a blessing, that there shall not be room enough to receive it.
-Malachi. 3:10

Acceptable and Profitable Services

There is always an acceptable and profitable way of serving God, as God is a rewarder not a task master.

(1.)   Serve willingly:

² Speak unto the children of Israel, that they bring me an offering: of every man that giveth it willingly with his heart ye shall take my offering.
-Exodus 25:2

⁶ For the LORD knoweth the way of the righteous: but the way of the ungodly shall perish.
-Psalm 1:6

(2.)   Serve with joy:

¹ Make a joyful noise unto the LORD, all ye lands. ² Serve the LORD with gladness: come before his presence with singing.
-Psalm 100:1-2

(3.)   Serve with obedience**:**

¹¹ If they obey and serve him, they shall spend their days in prosperity, and their years in pleasures.
-Job 36:11

(4.)   Serve with a diligent heart: God rewards only heart services not eye service.

¹³ Wherefore the Lord said, Forasmuch as this people draw near me with their mouth, and with their lips do honour me, but have removed their heart far from me, and their fear toward me is taught by the precept of men.
-Isaiah 29:13

Benefits of Service

➢   Diligent reward:

17 And the seventy returned again with joy, saying, Lord, even the devils are subject unto us through thy name.
-Luke 10:17

18 For the scripture saith, Thou shalt not muzzle the ox that treadeth out the corn. And, The labourer is worthy of his reward.
-1 Timothy 5:18

➢   Prosperity:

6 Pray for the peace of Jerusalem: they shall prosper that love thee.
-Psalm 122:6

11 If they obey and serve him, they shall spend their days in prosperity, and their years in pleasures.
-Job 36:11

➢   Blessings:

25 And ye shall serve the LORD your God, and he shall bless thy bread, and thy water; and I will take sickness away from the midst of thee.
-Exodus 23:25

➢ Total health, long life and protection.

²⁶ There shall nothing cast their young, nor be barren, in thy land: the number of thy days I will fulfill.
-Exodus 23:26

Kingdom addiction establishes kingdom addition. There is dignity in labour because the gateway to service is the pathway to greatness.

Chapter 6

COVENANT OF FINANCIAL PROSPERITY

God's wish for every covenant practitioner is prosperity.

² Beloved, I wish above all things that thou mayest prosper and be in health, even as thy soul prospereth.
-3 John 1:2

Prosperity in the kingdom does not come by strength or labour; it comes by grace and favour.

¹⁸ But thou shalt remember the LORD thy God: for it is he that giveth thee power to get wealth, that he may establish his covenant which he sware unto thy fathers, as it is this day.
-Deuteronomy 8:18

You are not born again to be poor again. Poverty is not Christianity. Poverty is not a sign of righteousness. Take the earth and give me heaven is a testimony of average men. There are two types of Christian, the **Abrahamic Christian** and the **Lazaroic Christian**. We all know that Abraham was a prosperous man on earth and still made heaven, but Lazarus on the other hand was an epitome of poverty on the earth but finally made heaven. But I choose to be the **Abrahamic Christian**. What is the value of long life if prosperity is not inclusive? One of the most destructive social vices is poverty. Eating well makes healthy, eating well makes strong, eating well guarantee long life, but eating well takes good money, see what the bible says

5 Who satisfieth thy mouth with good things; so that thy youth is renewed like the eagle's.
- Psalm 103:5

You need to embrace God's kind of prosperity and eschew poverty. Because after all *"The silver is mine, and the gold is mine, saith the LORD of hosts."* —Haggai 2:8

Every treasure of the earth belongs to God and Christ has paid the prize for your poverty and if you are still in poverty it is your fault.

9 For ye know the grace of our Lord Jesus Christ, that, though he was rich, yet for your sakes he became poor, that ye through his poverty might be rich.
-2 Corinthians 8:9

PATTERN OF PROSPERITY

He prospers the work of your hand

3 And he shall be like a tree planted by the rivers of water, that bringeth forth his fruit in his season; his leaf also shall not wither; and whatsoever he doeth shall prosper.
-Psalm 1:3

The work of our hand is the primary channel through which God blesses. So if you are not a worker, you are not a candidate for prosperity. If your hands are idle, God has a problem of finding how to bless you.

4 The sluggard will not plow by reason of the cold; therefore shall he beg in harvest, and have nothing.
-Proverbs 20:4

He enables the flow of divine ideas

1Behold, I will send my messenger, and he shall prepare the way before me: and the Lord, whom ye seek, shall suddenly come to his temple, even the messenger of the covenant, whom ye delight in: behold, he shall come, saith the LORD of hosts.
-Malachi 3:1

37 Jacob took him rods of green poplar, and of the hazel and chesnut tree; and pilled white strakes in them, and made the white appear which was in the rods.

38 And he set the rods which he had pilled before the flocks in the gutters in the watering troughs when the flocks came to drink, that they should conceive when they came to drink.

39 And the flocks conceived before the rods, and brought forth cattle ringstraked, speckled, and spotted.

-Genesis 30:37-39

Divine favour

21 And I will give this people favour in the sight of the Egyptians: and it shall come to pass, that, when ye go, ye shall not go empty:

-Exodus 3:21

36 And it shall come to pass, when your children shall say unto you, What mean ye by this service?

-Exodus 12:36

Patience

*15 But that on the good ground are they, which in
an honest and good heart, having heard the
word, keep it, and bring forth fruit with
patience.*
-Luke 8:15

Faithfulness

*11 If therefore ye have not been faithful in the
unrighteous mammon, who will commit to
your trust the true riches?*
-Luke 16:11

Before you become a heavy weight champion, you
need to engage in a heavy weight exercise, there is
always what to do in the secret in order to show in
the open.

Why Financial Prosperity

(a.)   As a proof of redemption

*12 Saying with a loud voice, Worthy is the Lamb
that was slain to receive power, and riches,
and wisdom, and strength, and honour, and
glory, and blessing.*
-Revelation 5:12

Immediately you give your life to Christ, son-ship
is activated. You begin to enjoy your father's
wealth.

*8 The silver is mine, and the gold is mine, saith
the LORD of hosts.*
-Haggai 2:8

(b.)   To be a blessing to the world.

*17 Charge them that are rich in this world, that
they be not highminded, nor trust in uncertain
riches, but in the living God, who giveth us richly
all things to enjoy;
18 That they do good, that they be rich in good
works, ready to distribute, willing to
communicate;
19 Laying up in store for themselves a good
foundation against the time to come, that they
may lay hold on eternal life.*
-1 Timothy 6:17-19

The reason God blesses you is for you to be a blessing to the world, God want you to be a channel not a container. **Channels flow, Container sting.** You need to understand that you are a care-taker of anything you have and the rightful owner is God.

*24 There is that scattereth, and yet increaseth;
and there is that withholdeth more than is meet,
but it tendeth to poverty.
25 The liberal soul shall be made fat: and he that
watereth shall be watered also himself.*
-Proverbs 11:24-25

¹ Cast thy bread upon the waters: for thou shalt find it after many days.
-Ecclesiastes 11:1

(c) To expand the kingdom of God.

¹⁷ Cry yet, saying, Thus saith the LORD of hosts; My cities through prosperity shall yet be spread abroad; and the LORD shall yet comfort Zion, and shall yet choose Jerusalem.
-Zechariah 1:17

The reason God is blessing you is so you continue to expand His kingdom here on earth. Let your finance get to where you cannot go.

(d) To help the poor.

¹¹ For the poor shall never cease out of the land: therefore I command thee, saying, Thou shalt open thane hand wide unto thy brother, to thy poor, and to thy needy, in thy land.
-Deuteronomy 15:11

²⁷ He that giveth unto the poor shall not lack: but he that hideth his eyes shall have many a curse.
-Proverbs 28:27

¹⁷ He that hath pity upon the poor lendeth unto the LORD; and that which he hath given will he pay him again.
-Proverbs 19:17

Scriptural Obligation for Financial Prosperity

(a.)   Tithing.

8 Will a man rob God? Yet ye have robbed me. But ye say, Wherein have we robbed thee? In tithes and offerings.
9 Ye are cursed with a curse: for ye have robbed me, even this whole nation.
10 Bring ye all the tithes into the storehouse, that there may be meat in mine house, and prove me now herewith, saith the LORD of hosts, if I will not open you the windows of heaven, and pour you out a blessing, that there shall not be room enough to receive it.
-Malachi 3:8-10,

30 And all the tithe of the land, whether of the seed of the land, or of the fruit of the tree, is the LORD'S: it is holy unto the LORD.
31 And if a man will at all redeem ought of his tithes, he shall add thereto the fifth part thereof.
-Leviticus 27:30-31

We all tithe—to God or the devil. Now, the question is, to whom do you pay to? Covenant tithing is 10% of your earning but the one for the devil has no percentage he can decide to take 200%. Covenant tithing is the acknowledgement to God that you have received His blessing and that you are qualified for another.

The benefit of tithing cannot be overemphasized. No matter how sweet a mango fruit maybe, you cannot eat the seed because when you eat the seed the generation of the fruit is over. Imagine everybody eating the seed of a mango, maybe there will not be any mango in the world again. Eating your tithe is like eating your seed. Eat your fruit, not your seed. Tithe is spiritual and it's not for carnal people.

(b) Worship offering.

16 Three times in a year shall all thy males appear before the lord thy God in the place which he shall choose; in the feast of unleavened bread, and in the feast of weeks, and in the feast of tabernacles: and they shall not appear before the lord empty.
-Deuteronomy 16:16

Giving is living. You must give. Poor people don't give. Rich people don't give. Only givers give. Until you sacrifice you can't be satisfied. Even God is a giver.

16 For God so loved the world, that he gave his only begotten Son, that whosoever believeth in him should not perish, but have everlasting life.
-John 3:16

God is a covenant keeper. He always keeps His promises. Every time you play your part God is always ready to do the rest. God is the same today, tomorrow and forever.

Chapter 7

ENDOWMENT WITH POWER

Holy Ghost Baptism

The time of God the father is gone. God the son is gone. We are in the era of God the spirit.

24 God is a Spirit: and they that worship him must worship him in spirit and in truth.
-John 4:24

7 Nevertheless I tell you the truth; It is expedient for you that I go away: for if I go not away, the Comforter will not come unto you; but if I depart, I will send him unto you.
-John 16:7

8 But ye shall receive power, after that the Holy Ghost is come upon you: and ye shall be witnesses unto me both in Jerusalem, and in all Judaea, and in Samaria, and unto the uttermost part of the earth.
-Acts 1:8

The Holy Spirit is one of the God's personalities in the Godhead. The Holy Ghost is the person which you cannot see that is why He is called "**Ghost**" but holy one. He is not a feeling, but He has feeling. He has emotions. All throughout scriptures, the Holy Ghost is referred to as "HE."

26 But the Comforter, which is the Holy Ghost, whom the Father will send in my name, he shall teach you all things, and bring all things to your remembrance, whatsoever I have said unto you.
-John 14:26

13 Howbeit when he, the Spirit of truth, is come, he will guide you into all truth: for he shall not speak of himself; but whatsoever he shall hear, that shall he speak: and he will shew you things to come.
-John 16:13

If you must succeed in life, you need the Holy Spirit and His baptism in all area of your life. You must be hungry and thirsty for divine help.

Who is the Holy Ghost

- He is a person not feeling or influence.
- He is the comforter.
- He is the third person in the Godhead.
- He is the promised of the Father.

5 For John truly baptized with water; but ye shall be baptized with the Holy Ghost not many days hence.
-Acts 1:5

- He is the divine force behind creation.

² And the earth was without form, and void; and darkness was upon the face of the deep. And the Spirit of God moved upon the face of the waters.
-Genesis 1:2

³⁰ Thou sendest forth thy spirit, they are created: and thou renewest the face of the earth.
-Psalm 104:30.

- The Holy Spirit is the power that works in us for answer to our prayers.

²⁰ Now unto him that is able to do exceeding abundantly above all that we ask or think, according to the power that worketh in us, ²¹ Unto him be glory in the church by Christ Jesus throughout all ages, world without end. Amen.
-Ephesians 3:20-21

²⁶ Likewise the Spirit also helpeth our infirmities: for we know not what we should pray for as we ought: but the Spirit itself maketh intercession for us with groanings which cannot be uttered.
-Romans 8:26

- He converts people from their sins and lead them to salvation.

⁷ Nevertheless I tell you the truth; It is expedient for you that I go away: for if I go not away, the Comforter will not come unto you; but if I depart, I will send him unto you.

8 And when he is come, he will reprove the world of sin, and of righteousness, and of judgment: 9 Of sin, because they believe not on me.
-John 16:7-9

3 Wherefore I give you to understand, that no man speaking by the Spirit of God calleth Jesus accursed: and that no man can say that Jesus is the Lord, but by the Holy Ghost.
-1 Corinthians 12:3

16 The Spirit itself beareth witness with our spirit, that we are the children of God.
-Romans 8:16.

- He impacts divine enablement.

8 But ye shall receive power, after that the Holy Ghost is come upon you: and ye shall be witnesses unto me both in Jerusalem, and in all Judaea, and in Samaria, and unto the uttermost part of the earth.
-Acts 1:8

- He is a teacher of all things.

26 But the Comforter, which is the Holy Ghost, whom the Father will send in my name, he shall teach you all things, and bring all things to your remembrance, whatsoever I have said unto you.
-John 14:26

²⁷ But the anointing which ye have received of him abideth in you, and ye need not that any man teach you: but as the same anointing teacheth you of all things, and is truth, and is no lie, and even as it hath taught you, ye shall abide in him.
-1 John 2:27

- He is our counselor and guide.

¹⁴ For as many as are led by the Spirit of God, they are the sons of God.

¹⁵ For ye have not received the spirit of bondage again to fear; but ye have received the Spirit of adoption, whereby we cry, Abba, Father.

¹⁶ The Spirit itself beareth witness with our spirit, that we are the children of God:
-Romans 8:14-16

¹³ Howbeit when he, the Spirit of truth, is come, he will guide you into all truth: for he shall not speak of himself; but whatsoever he shall hear,thatshall he speak: and he will shew you things to come.
-John 16:13

- He speaks.

²⁶ Likewise the Spirit also helpeth our infirmities: for we know not what we should pray for as we

ought: but the Spirit itself maketh intercession for us with groanings which cannot be uttered. ²⁷ And he that searcheth the hearts knoweth what is the mind of the Spirit, because he maketh intercession for the saints according to the will of God.
-Romans 8:26-27

² As they ministered to the Lord, and fasted, the Holy Ghost said, Separate me Barnabas and Saul for the work whereunto I have called them.
-Acts 13:2.

Ministry of the Holy Spirit

- He makes people to be born again.

⁵ Jesus answered, Verily, verily, I say unto thee, Except a man be born of water and of the Spirit, he cannot enter into the kingdom of God. ⁶ That which is born of the flesh is flesh; and that which is born of the Spirit is spirit. ⁷ Marvel not that I said unto thee, Ye must be born again.
-John 3:5-7

- He reproves the world of sin, righteousness and judgment.

⁸ And when he is come, he will reprove the world of sin, and of righteousness, and of judgment: ⁹ Of sin, because they believe not on me.
-John 16:8-9

- He cast out devils.

28 Verily I say unto you, There be some standing here, which shall not taste of death, till they see the Son of man coming in his kingdom.
-Matthews 12:28

- He grants us understanding into the scripture.

10 But God hath revealed them unto us by his Spirit: for the Spirit searcheth all things, yea, the deep things of God.
-1 Corinthians 2:10

The Person Nature of the Holy Spirit in the Scripture

- The Bible continually used personal pronoun to refer to the Holy Spirit.

26 But when the Comforter is come, whom I will send unto you from the Father, even the Spirit of truth, which proceedeth from the Father, he shall testify of me.
-John 15:26

7 Nevertheless I tell you the truth; it is expedient for you that I go away: for if I go not away, the

Comforter will not come unto you; but if I depart, I will send him unto you.
8 And when he is come, he will reprove the world of sin, and of righteousness, and of judgment.
-John 16:7-8

- The Holy Spirit speaks.

2 As they ministered to the Lord, and fasted, the Holy Ghost said, Separate me Barnabas and Saul for the work whereunto I have called them.
-Act 13:2

7 He that hath an ear, let him hear what the Spirit saith unto the churches; To him that overcometh will I give to eat of the tree of life, which is in the midst of the paradise of God.
-Revelation 2:7

- He helps our weaknesses.

26 Likewise the Spirit also helpeth our infirmities: for we know not what we should pray for as we ought: but the Spirit itself maketh intercession for us with groanings which cannot be uttered.
-Romans 8:26

- He has emotion.

27 And he that searcheth the hearts knoweth what is the mind of the Spirit, because he maketh

intercession for the saints according to the will of God.
-Romans 8:27

- He is a teacher.

27 But the anointing which ye have received of him abideth in you, and ye need not that any man teach you: but as the same anointing teacheth you of all things, and is truth, and is no lie, and even as it hath taught you, ye shall abide in him.
-1 John 2:27

- He is our guide.

13 Howbeit when he, the Spirit of truth, is come, he will guide you into all truth: for he shall not speak of himself; but whatsoever he shall hear, that shall he speak: and he will shew you things to come.
-John 16:13

- He calls people to the work of God.

2 As they ministered to the Lord, and fasted, the Holy Ghost said, Separate me Barnabas and Saul for the work whereunto I have called them.
-Acts 13:2

Why Every Believer must be Baptize with the Holy Spirit

- It is the sign that must follow all believers.

17 And these signs shall follow them that believe; In my name shall they cast out devils; they shall speak with new tongues.
-Mark 16:17.

- To be empowered for effective witnessing.

3 To whom also he shewed himself alive after his passion by many infallible proofs, being seen of them forty days, and speaking of the things pertaining to the kingdom of God.
-Acts 1:3

- It is the foundation for the manifestation of the fullness of the power of the Holy Spirit.

31 And when they had prayed, the place was shaken where they were assembled together; and they were all filled with the Holy Ghost, and they spake the word of God with boldness.
32 And the multitude of them that believed were of one heart and of one soul: neither said any of them that ought of the things which he possessed was his own; but they had all things common.
33 And with great power gave the apostles witness of the resurrection of the Lord Jesus: and great grace was upon them all.
-Acts 4:31-33

- It is for communication with the father.

2 For he that speaketh in an unknown tongue speaketh not unto men, but unto God: for no man understandeth him; howbeit in the spirit he speaketh mysteries.
-1 Corinthians 14:2

It is the speaking of mystery in the spirit. Generally, the Holy Spirit baptism is the experience of the infilling of the spirit of God with evidence of speaking in tongues.

4 And they were all filled with the Holy Ghost, and began to speak with other tongues, as the Spirit gave them utterance.
-Acts 2:4

- It is the promise of the father.

29 But they constrained him, saying, Abide with us: for it is toward evening, and the day is far spent. And he went in to tarry with them.
-Luke 24:29

26 But when the Comforter is come, whom I will send unto you from the Father, even the Spirit of truth, which proceedeth from the Father, he shall testify of me.
-John 15:26

¹¹ He answered and said unto them, Because it is given unto you to know the mysteries of the kingdom of heaven, but to them it is not given.
-Matthew 3:11

- It is for victorious and fulfilled Christian living.

⁸ But ye shall receive power, after that the Holy Ghost is come upon you: and ye shall be witnesses unto me both in Jerusalem, and in all Judaea, and in Samaria, and unto the uttermost part of the earth.
-Acts 1:8

⁷ Nevertheless I tell you the truth; It is expedient for you that I go away: for if I go not away, the Comforter will not come unto you; but if I depart, I will send him unto you.
¹³ Howbeit when he, the Spirit of truth, is come, he will guide you into all truth: for he shall not speak of himself; but whatsoever he shall hear, that shall he speak: and he will shew you things to come.
¹⁴ John 16:14He shall glorify me: for he shall receive of mine, and shall shew it unto you.
¹⁵ John 16:15All things that the Father hath are mine: therefore said I, that he shall take of mine, and shall shew it unto you.
-John 16:7, 13-15

- It builds up your faith.

²⁰ But ye, beloved, building up yourselves on your most holy faith, praying in the Holy Ghost.
-Jude 1:20

How Can I be Baptized?

- You must be born again.

³⁷ Now when they heard this, they were pricked in their heart, and said unto Peter and to the rest of the apostles, Men and brethren, what shall we do?
³⁸ Then Peter said unto them, Repent, and be baptized every one of you in the name of Jesus Christ for the remission of sins, and ye shall receive the gift of the Holy Ghost.
³⁹ For the promise is unto you, and to your children, and to all that are afar off, even as many as the Lord our God shall call.
-Acts 2:37-39

- You must be desirous and thirsty for him.

³⁷ In the last day, that great day of the feast, Jesus stood and cried, saying, If any man thirst, let him come unto me, and drink.
-John 7:37

²⁴ The fear of the wicked, it shall come upon him: but the desire of the righteous shall be granted.
-Proverbs 10:24

- You must believe that the baptism of the Holy Spirit is for you.

³⁸ Then Peter said unto them, Repent, and be baptized every one of you in the name of Jesus Christ for the remission of sins, and ye shall receive the gift of the Holy Ghost.
³⁹ For the promise is unto you, and to your children, and to all that are afar off, even as many as the Lord our God shall call.
-Acts 2:38-39

- You must recognize that Jesus is the baptizer.

- You must trust and keep his word.

³⁸ He that believeth on me, as the scripture hath said, out of his belly shall flow rivers of living water.
-John 7:38

- You must ask for the baptism.

7 Ask, and it shall be given you; seek, and ye shall find; knock, and it shall be opened unto you:
-Matthew 7:7

- You must open your mouth and speak as the spirit prompt you.

4 And they were all filled with the Holy Ghost, and began to speak with other tongues, as the Spirit gave them utterance.
-Acts 2:4

Having been baptized, the only way to show that you are led by the spirit is through the display of the fruit of the spirit. The fruits include;
(1.)	Love.
(2.)	Joy.
(3.)	Peace.
(4.)	Patience.
(5.)	Kindness.
(6.)	Goodness.
(7.)	Faithfulness.
(8.)	Gentleness.
(9.)	Self-control.

All of these are the evidence of the fruit of the spirit. The Holy Spirit is the best thing that can happen to any believer. It gives meaning to human life.

Water Baptism

Immediately you give your life to Christ the next thing is water baptism.

16 He that believeth and is baptized shall be saved; but he that believeth not shall be damned.
-Mark 16:16

37 Now when they heard this, they were pricked in their heart, and said unto Peter and to the rest of the apostles, Men and brethren, what shall we do?

38 Then Peter said unto them, Repent, and be baptized every one of you in the name of Jesus Christ for the remission of sins, and ye shall receive the gift of the Holy Ghost.
-Acts 2:37-38

Water baptism is the physical demonstration of our spiritual identification with the death, burial and resurrection of Christ.

3 Know ye not, that so many of us as were baptized into Jesus Christ were baptized into his death?

4 Therefore we are buried with him by baptism into death: that like as Christ was raised up from the dead by the glory of the Father, even so we also should walk in newness of life.

7 For he that is dead is freed from sin.

-Romans 6:3-4, 7

Baptism doesn't save, salvation does. But water baptism is compulsory for every child of God.

What is Acceptable Water Baptism

- Genuine water baptism must be after salvation / repentance.

38 Then Peter said unto them, Repent, and be baptized every one of you in the name of Jesus Christ for the remission of sins, and ye shall receive the gift of the Holy Ghost.

-Acts 2:38

- It must be by immersion.

*37 And Philip said, If thou believest with all thane heart, thou mayest. And he answered and said, I believe that Jesus Christ is the Son of God.
38 And he commanded the chariot to stand still: and they went down both into the water, both Philip and the eunuch; and he baptized him.*
-Acts 8:37-38

16 And Jesus, when he was baptized, went up straightway out of the water: and, lo, the heavens were opened unto him, and he saw the Spirit of God descending like a dove, and lighting upon him:

-Matthew 3:16

There is no provision in the Bible for infant baptism.

Benefit of Water Baptism

- Access to God, open heaven.
- Seal of Son-ship
- Change of status, everything answers to you.

The pattern of baptism is repent before baptism.

37 Now when they heard this, they were pricked in their heart, and said unto Peter and to the rest of the apostles, Men and brethren, what shall we do?
38 Then Peter said unto them, Repent, and be baptized every one of you in the name of Jesus Christ for the remission of sins, and ye shall receive the gift of the Holy Ghost.
-Acts 2:37-38

Baptism requires coming up out of the water.

CONCLUSION

Your root determines your fruit and your light determines your height. Things do not just answer to personality, they answer to principle. Until you live for a cause you'd remain under a curse. God is only committed to what He commands, and those who seek to do extra-ordinary things end up not doing anything. However, you can choose to do ordinary things in an extra-ordinary way.

Labor is good but favor is better. There is difference between race and grace and that is what this book is talking about. Spirit don't run race they are engraced.

Christianity is a religion of simplicity, but complex people like you and I find it very different to understand. Right now, understand that the devil is not worried that you gave your life to Christ, but where he begins to have issue with you is when you begin to apply great principles such as outlined in this book.

For concerns, send an email to the author:
olabisipeter26@gmail.com